Look for these other
Cover-to-Cover chapter books!

The Elephant's Ancestors

Magic Tricks and More

Great Eagle and Small One

James Meets the Prairie

The Jesse Owens Story

Little Fish

What's New with Mr. Pizooti?

The Whooping Crane

Yankee Doodle and the Secret Society

What If You'd Been at Jamestown?

by Ellen Keller

Perfection Learning® CA

Cover Illustration: Dea Marks
Inside Illustrations: Dea Marks, Kay Ewald

About the Author

Ellen Keller is a former Minnesota teacher who now lives in New York City. She currently writes stories and learning games for children. Ms. Keller has visited many towns and cities in Europe as well as in Japan, Turkey, and India. One of her most interesting travel experiences ever was to visit the original site of Jamestown and then the nearby reconstructed settlement.

Image Credits: Library of Congress pp. 6, 8, 12, 13, 18, 21 top, 23, 24, 26, 28, 30, 31, 32, 35, 36, 37, 38, 42, 43, 44; National Portrait Gallery pp. 7, 49; *Theatrum Imperii Magnae Britanniae* p. 11; Bibliotheque Nationale p. 14; Association for the Preservation of Virginia Antiquities pp. 21 bottom, 39, 51, 52, 53, 54; *America, PART 1* p. 45; *Orbis Sensualium* p. 48

Perfection Learning® Corporation
1000 North Second Avenue, P.O. Box 500
Logan, Iowa 51546-1099.

Paperback ISBN 0-7891-2001-1
Cover Craft® ISBN 0-7807-6689-x

Table of Contents

Chapter I

The Plan

Long ago, there was no United States.
The Indians owned the land.

King James of England heard about this land. He wanted the land for himself.

King James I of England

The king knew the land belonged to the Indians. So he made a plan. The king would send men across the sea. They would lie to the Indians.

The men would say that they only wanted to look at the land. Then they would pretend to leave. But they would not leave! They would stay on the land.

The English planned to build a colony. They would name it for the king. They would call it Jamestown.

The king sent three ships. About 100 men and 5 boys made the trip. The ships carried supplies too.

King James I

8

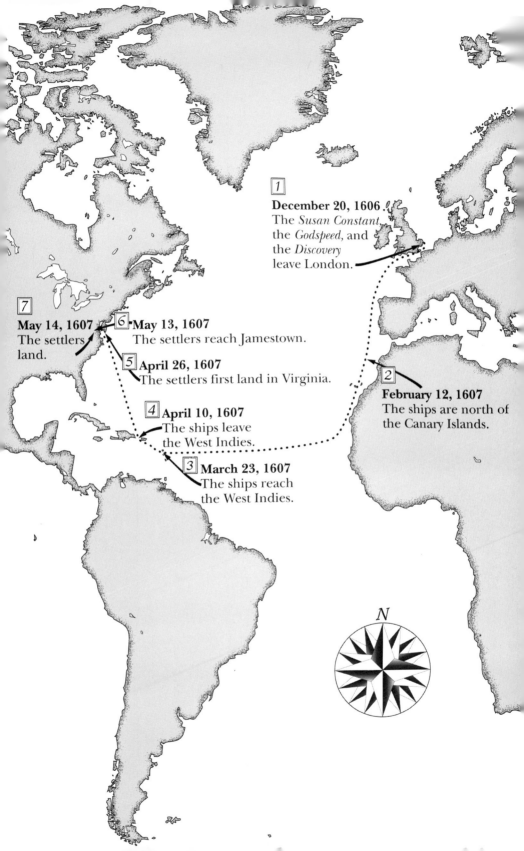

1 December 20, 1606.
The *Susan Constant*,
the *Godspeed*, and
the *Discovery*
leave London.

2 February 12, 1607
The ships are north of
the Canary Islands.

7 May 14, 1607
The settlers
land.

6 May 13, 1607
The settlers reach Jamestown.

5 April 26, 1607
The settlers first land in Virginia.

4 April 10, 1607
The ships leave
the West Indies.

3 March 23, 1607
The ships reach
the West Indies.

N

One boy was only ten years old. What if you were that boy? America was far away. You might never see England again.

Well, I was one of those five boys. It was both scary and fun for us. We were young. But we were treated like men.

Most of the men were called gentlemen. They were rich. They never did hard work. They had helpers to do it for them.

These men hoped to get richer in Jamestown. They wanted to find gold.

Others were not known as gentlemen. They knew how to do hard work.

Some were carpenters. Some were laborers. One was a doctor. And one was a barber. But none were farmers.

A NOBLE-MAN

A LADY

A GENTLE WOMAN

A GENTLE MAN

A CITIZEN

A CITIZENS WIFE

A COUNTRY WOMAN

A COUNTRY-MAN

Captain John
Smith (1580–1631)

There were also soldiers. One soldier was Captain John Smith. Captain Smith was younger than most of the others. But he had had many adventures. Smith had traveled to far-off places. Once he had been forced to be a slave.

Captain John Smith bragged about his feats. I liked to hear him talk. But some men hated him.

Chapter 2

The Trip

The trip lasted almost five months. It was a hard time for us.

We ran out of food and water. Many people got sick. Some died.

I was one of the lucky ones. I didn't get sick.

Fear filled the men's hearts. Some believed in sea monsters. Others believed in evil spirits.

How would you have felt? You might have been hungry or sick. You might have been homesick.

Then the great day came. "Land ho!"

Cries of joy rose from the three ships. At last, we could see land. Everything would be all right.

Chapter 3

The New Land

We could not believe our eyes. The
land was beautiful. White flowers
covered the trees. Everything was fresh
and green.

We wouldn't be hungry anymore. There were animals everywhere. Fish filled the rivers and streams. Fresh water flowed.

We came to shore. But we were not alone. We were being watched.

Deep in the forest, eyes watched our every move. These eyes belonged to the Powhatan Indians. This was their land.

Chapter 4

The Indians

The Indians had seen white men
before. They had come from across the
sea. They had traded beads and pots for
food. Then they had left.

So the Indians thought we were traders. They hoped we would trade the mighty thundersticks that we called guns. No one had ever traded those before.

The Indians watched us from their hiding places. We ate, washed, and rested. The other boys and I swam in the sea. We ran up and down the beach.

All the while, the eyes followed us.

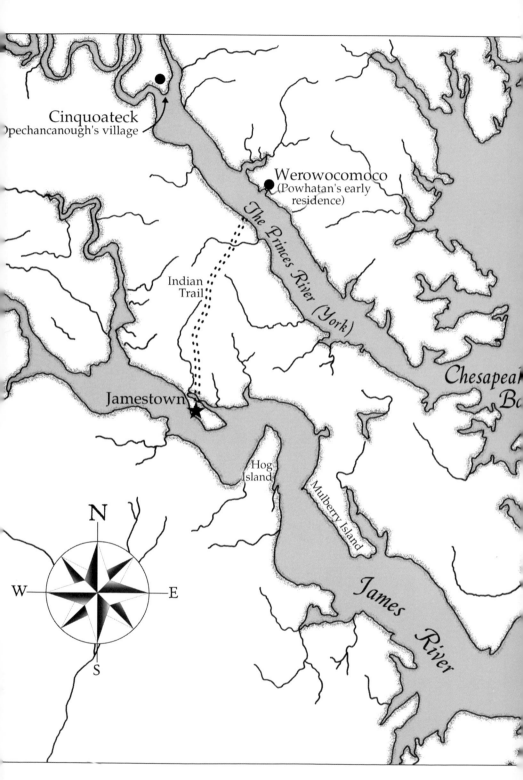

Cinquoateck
Opechancanough's village

Werowocomoco
(Powhatan's early
residence)

The Princes River (York)

Indian
Trail

Jamestown

Hog
Island

Mulberry Island

Chesapeake
Bay

James River

N
W   E
S

After a time, the Indians came out.
They asked us to visit their village. It
was one of many
Powhatan villages.

We had fun. We
watched dances
and ate good food.

In return, we
gave beads to the
Indians. They
thought the beads
were beautiful.

Glass trading beads
found at the Jamestown site

After a few days, we boarded the ships. We sailed up the river. There we found what we were looking for. We found a place to build Jamestown.

Chapter 5

Jamestown

It was May of 1607. We began
building Jamestown. The other boys and
I worked hard. We cut down trees for a
wall. It went around the town.

Soon, trouble began. The gentlemen weren't used to hard work. They didn't want to help. They wanted to look for gold.

Then June and July came. It was hot! We got sick. Many died.

We were building Jamestown on a
swamp. But we didn't know it.
The water in the summer
was harmful. Bugs
were everywhere.
They carried a
deadly illness.

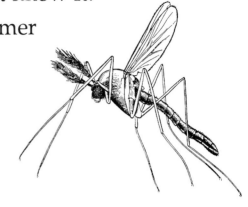

Summer ended.
Only about half of

Mosquito

us were still alive. Very few of
the houses were done.

There weren't any farmers. So crops hadn't been planted. And soon food was almost gone.

That wasn't all. We also had trouble with our leader. He stole extra food for himself. And he ordered us to build him a castle.

The men were angry. They threw the leader in jail.

We named Captain John Smith as our new leader. Even though he bragged a lot. And he thought he was better than anyone else.

But John Smith was good for us. He didn't care what others thought of him. He knew what had to be done.

Things quickly changed. Captain Smith made rules.

Making lumber

And he punished those who didn't follow his rules.

The Indians helped us. They brought food. They told us to cut the tall grass where the bugs hid.

Captain Smith spent time with the Indians. He learned their words. He wrote them down. He knew it was important to know and speak their language.

Indian drawings showing enemy warriors

Chapter 6

Powhatan

By December of 1607, the food was almost gone. So Captain Smith visited Indian villages. He traded for food.

The captain took 20 men and me. I was excited. But I was also scared. How would you have felt?

We visited two or three villages. We traded.

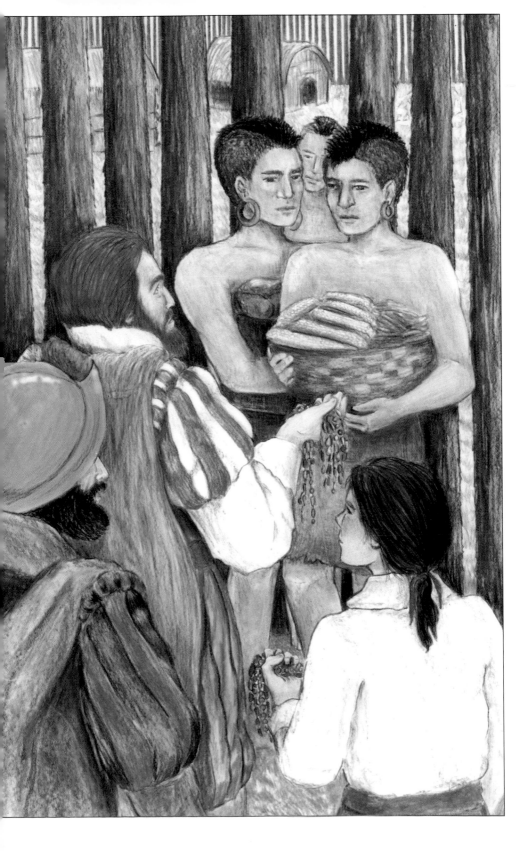

An Indian village

Then one night, something terrible happened.

How they tooke him prisoner in the Oaze 1607.

C. Smith bindeth a saluage to his arme fighteth with the King of Pamaunkee and all his company, and slew 3 of them.

Capture of Captain John Smith

We were sitting around the fire. Indians leaped from the darkness and grabbed us. They dragged us before their great chief Powhatan. He was the leader of all the Indians.

Powhatan knew about us. But he had never met any of us.

Within the image:

King Powhatan comands C. Smith to be slaine, his daughter Pokahontas beggs his life his thankfullneß and how he subiected 39 of their kings. reade ẏ history.

printed by Iames Reeue

John Smith's capture by Powhatan

Powhatan knew most of us were grown men. But still we couldn't feed ourselves in a land filled with food.

He knew we had chosen the worst spot to camp. It was a swamp of harm and death.

Powhatan had heard about Captain John Smith too. He knew Captain Smith was different from the other men. Powhatan thought that Captain Smith was brave and proud.

Powhatan wanted to know about the captain's magic.

Captain Smith had a ball with a moving point. It always pointed north. The ball was a compass. The Indians had never seen one before.

Powhatan and Captain Smith admired each other. But each wanted power over the other.

Powhatan liked how Captain Smith had learned the Indian language. It made Powhatan want to trust John Smith.

Captain Smith wanted to trust Powhatan too. So he left me in Powhatan's village. He did it to show good faith. He also wanted me to learn their language and ways.

Indians planting fields

Chapter 7

Life in the Village

Think about how I felt. I wanted to be brave. But it was hard.

Time passed. I felt more at home.

I helped clear land for planting. I helped prepare land for new houses that the women built. Some of the houses were 40 yards long.

The food was good. And there was more than enough for everyone.

Spearfishing

Drying fish over a fire

The Indians treated me with kindness. They helped me learn their ways.

I liked my new friends. But I thought they did some strange things.

The Indians washed in the river every day. We believed that taking too many baths made a person weak. The Indians thought we smelled bad. And we probably did!

I learned to hunt deer. We hid behind trees and watched the animals. One boy wore a deer head. He carried a deerskin over his arm. It made the deer come closer.

At night, we returned to the village. Everyone was proud of the deer we brought back.

I felt strong and proud too. I learned that hunters were the richest and most powerful members of the tribe.

Some women were also powerful. They knew how to grow huge crops. Some were even leaders. They were as powerful as the men.

I learned a lot from the Indians. They were like my family.

Powhatan had about 100 children. His favorite was his daughter Pocahontas. But he had a special love for me. I had become one of his family.

The settlers and Indians got along quite well. They traded. They visited each other's villages.

Cut pieces of copper used in trade with the Indians. Found at the Jamestown site.

There were a few problems. But the two groups worked them out.

Soon, more Jamestown boys stayed in the villages. And some Indian boys stayed in Jamestown.

The leader often sent Pocahontas to Jamestown. Other Indian girls and boys went with her. Sometimes they took food. Sometimes they carried messages.

Pocahontas and the others ran races
with the Jamestown boys. The boys
taught the Indians how to turn
cartwheels. Both groups learned each
other's language.

This was one of the best times for us.
Would you have liked to learn and play
with the Indians?

Chapter 8

More Settlers

NOVA BRITANNIA.

OFFERING MOST

Excellent fruites by Planting in VIRGINIA.

Exciting all such as be well affected to further the same.

LONDON
Printed for SAMVEL MACHAM, and are to be sold at his Shop in Pauls Church-yard, at the Signe of the Bul-head.
1609.

As time passed, more boats came. They were filled with settlers. By fall of 1609, there were about 500 settlers in Jamestown. Now there were also women and children.

An English booklet printed in 1609 urged people to settle in Virginia.

Captain Smith objected to the people
who came. Most didn't know how to
work. Building was slow. And there was
never enough food.

In September, Captain Smith got hurt.
He returned to England. He planned to
come back to Jamestown. But he never
did.

Thomas West, leader after John Smith

A new leader was chosen. The new leader and Powhatan did not get along.

Many people hated living in Jamestown. Many still wanted to find gold. But they never did.

Chapter 9

The Starving Time

The winter of 1609 would be known as "the starving time." It was one of the most horrible times in early America.

Powhatan knew that we would never leave the land. So the Indians tried to make us leave.

They stopped giving us food. When we left the fort, the Indians shot arrows at us.

We were
starving.
Many people
died. We dug
roots to eat.
We ate snakes,
rats, dogs, and horses. We grew weak.
During the cold winter, we needed
firewood. So
we broke
apart our
houses. And
we broke apart the
wall around the fort.
Still, many settlers froze.

Spring came. We decided to leave
Jamestown. We boarded the ship and
sailed down the river. Finally, we were
going home to England!

What if you had been one of the
settlers? How would you have felt?

Partway down the river, we saw another ship. It carried a new leader, more settlers, and food. So we returned to Jamestown.

The new leader was firm. Everyone had to work hard. The new leader fought wars with the Indians. And soon, the settlers began winning.

The number of settlers grew. They took more land from the Indians. They started more colonies. They learned to farm. They built schools. And they learned to survive the winters.

Years later, Pocahontas married a settler. For the first time, the Indians and the English tried to live in peace.

Ætatis suæ 21. Aº. 1616.

ioaks als Rebecka daughter to the mighty Prince
vhatan Emperour of Attanoughkomouck als Virginia
werted and baptized in the Christian faith, and
Wife to the wor"! M" Tho: Rolff.

Pocahontas after her marriage to John Rolfe

Chapter 10

Jamestown Today

Jamestown is remembered as America's first colony.

Visiting Jamestown can help you imagine what it was like in 1607. Jamestown is cared for by the National Park Service. The Association for the Preservation of Virginia Antiquities (APVA) helps too.

You can visit the actual site of the fort. Brick outlines of some of the houses remain. There are also the ruins of an old church tower.

Jamestown dig site

Today scientists are digging up parts of Jamestown. In 1996, they found part of the original fort. It was thought that the fort walls had been washed away by the James River.

Jug found at the Jamestown site

Jamestown dig site showing the fort wall

The fort was the shape of a triangle. Two sides were 300 feet long. That's the length of a football field. The third side was 420 feet long. There was about an acre of land inside the walls.

Scientists also have found artifacts dating back to 1607 and before. An artifact is something that was made by a human. These include swords, armor, jewelry, pottery, and coins.

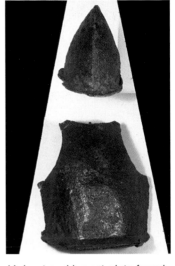

Helmet and breast plate found at Jamestown

Scientists have found an old grave. In it was the skeleton of a male settler.

The scientists plan to study the bones. They hope to learn more about the people of Jamestown.

A scientist digging up the skeleton of a settler at Jamestown

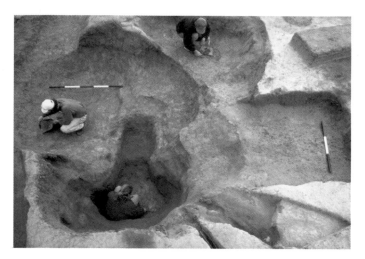

Pit at Jamestown where some objects were found

A scientist digging up a candlestick at Jamestown

The cleaned brass candlestick

The APVA hopes to finish the digging by 2007. That will be the 400th anniversary of the arrival of the first settlers.

Likenesses of the settlement and a Powhatan village have been built. You can visit the houses. You can see where the people lived. See how they lived.

Also, the ships that brought the settlers have been rebuilt. You can board these ships and imagine what it was like to sail to a new land.

You can see the woods as they were in 1607. Are Indians still watching from the trees?

You can learn a lot about Jamestown by visiting museums and visitor centers. The museums hold many of the artifacts. The visitor centers have exhibits, maps, and models of the area.

Jamestown today tells the story of the people who helped make the first history of colonial America—the language, the politics, the trading, and much of the culture.

If you want to learn more about Jamestown, write

Outreach Education Department
Jamestown-Yorktown Foundation
P.O. Box 1607
Williamsburg, VA 23187-1607.